English

A REFERENCE FOR STUDENTS AND PARENTS

by Roxane Fox

illustrated by Andrea Champlin

SCHOLASTIC INC.

New York Toronto London Auckland Sydney
Mexico City New Delhi Hong Kong Buenos Aires

ISBN 0-439-67205-8

12 11 10 9 8 7 6 5 4 3 2 5 6 7 8 9/0

Printed in the U.S.A. 66

First Scholastic printing, September 2004

Cover and interior pages designed by: Bob Filipowich
Developed and produced by: WWK Consulting Group, Inc., 201 West 70th Street, New York, NY 10023

NOTE TO PARENTS

Helping children do their homework successfully requires some planning. Study habits and time management are important skills for children to learn. The following tips may give you and your child strategies for doing homework more efficiently. Both you and your child will learn to survive English homework!

- Have your child do homework immediately after coming home from school. A quick snack is okay, but any other activity should wait until later.
- Make sure your child has a quiet, well-lit place to work.
- Help your child gather the materials necessary for his or her homework. Remember to have enough pencils, paper, and other tools ready.
- Try to schedule after-school activities on days when there is not as much homework.
- Long-term projects take planning. Encourage your child to work on a project in small sections, rather than tackle it all in one evening.
- Make sure your child has read a book for a book report before the writing is due to begin.
- Children need encouragement and reassurance. Patience and praise help children to become better students.

CHAPTER 1

A Look at Letters and Languages

The **English language** uses the **Roman alphabet**. There are many other alphabets used throughout the world. For instance, to write words in the Russian language, the Cyrillic alphabet is used. Words in Cyrillic are written and read from left to right. Some alphabets, such as Hebrew, Japanese, Arabic, and Chinese, are written and read from right to left.

The study of language is called **linguistics**. People who study language are **linguists**.

People who study **grammar**, the rules for speaking and writing a language, are called **grammarians**.

Phoneticians study **phonetics**, or the sound elements of a spoken language.

Semanticians study **semantics**, the meanings of words and word parts, and how a language changes from place to place and through time.

The maps on page 6 show where the five most common languages are spoken.

FIVE MOST COMMON LANGUAGES

Language	Number of Speakers
Chinese (dialects)	over 1,025,000,000
English	over 497,000,000
Hindi	about 476,000,000
Spanish	about 409,000,000
Arabic	about 235,000,000

(Note: Figures are taken from 1998 *World Almanac*.)

English

French

Spanish

Dutch

Hebrew

Arabic

LANGUAGES SPOKEN AROUND THE WORLD

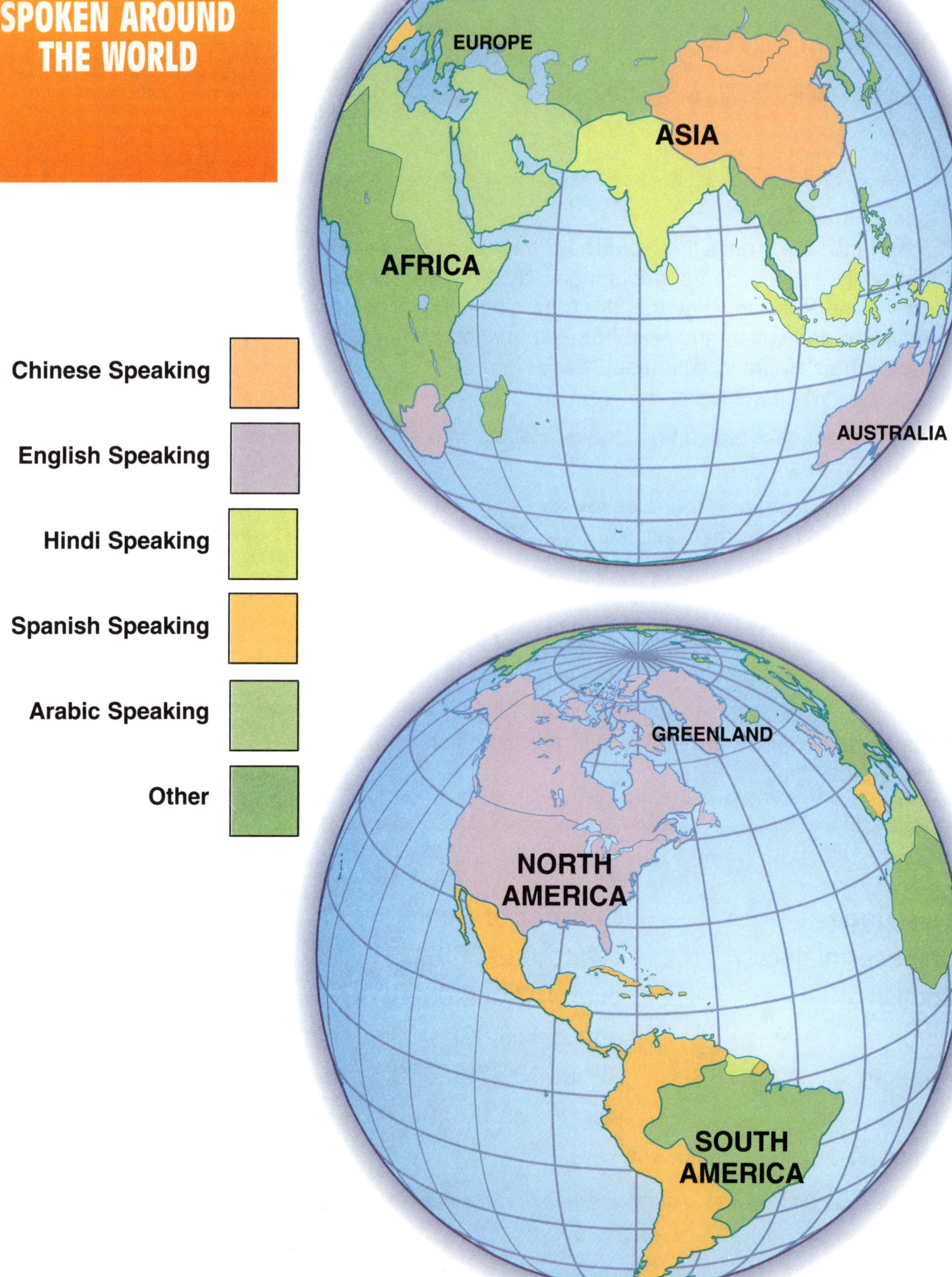

CHAPTER 2

What's That Sound?

CONSONANTS

The English alphabet has 26 letters. Five of the letters—**a**, **e**, **i**, **o**, and **u**—are **vowels**. The rest are **consonants**. **Y** is the only letter of the alphabet that can be either a vowel or a consonant, depending on its sound in a word. If **y** has a vowel sound (for example, *e* as in *fairy* or *i* as in *sky*), it's considered a vowel. **Y** in words such as *yard* and *year* is a consonant.

a b c d
e f g h
i j k l
m n o
p q r s
t u v w
x y z

CONSONANTS

A **consonant blend** is two or more consonants whose sounds can be blended together. Consonant blends can appear at the beginning, middle, or end of words.

- If a blend is at the beginning of a word, it's called an **initial blend**.

  drive

- If a blend is in the middle of a word, it's called a **medial blend**.

  En**gl**ish

- If a blend is at the end of a word, it's called a **final blend**.

  wa**sp**

THREE MAIN FAMILIES OF INITIAL BLENDS

r blends

grass **tr**ee **br**ide **cr**ate **dr**ive **fr**ame

l blends

place **bl**ood **cl**ock **fl**ower **gl**ue

s blends

swing **sp**eed **sk**y **sl**ipper **sn**ow **st**eep

Use paper to write words with initial, medial, and final blends.

CONSONANTS
VOWELS

A **consonant digraph** is two consonants that combine to make one new sound.

thick **sh**ape **ph**one **ch**ange

Some words end with consonant digraphs.

wi**th** wi**sh**

A **consonant cluster** is three consonants together in one syllable of a word.

thrill pa**tch** **spl**ash

VOWELS

A **vowel pair** is two vowels together that form one long vowel sound. Usually, the first vowel in the pair stands for the long vowel sound and the next vowel is silent.

Some vowel pairs:

g**oa**t fr**ee** t**ie**

A **vowel digraph** is two vowels together that form either a long or a short vowel sound. A vowel digraph sometimes has a special sound of its own, such as the *oo* sound in *school.*

Some vowel digraphs:

br**ea**d fr**ei**ght **au**thor
short long short

A vowel paired with **w** sometimes makes a vowel sound, as in the words *fawn* and *awful.*

A **diphthong** contains two vowels blended together to make one new sound. When a vowel is paired with **w**, the pair sometimes makes a new vowel sound like the **ow** in *gown.*

oil t**oy** g**ow**n

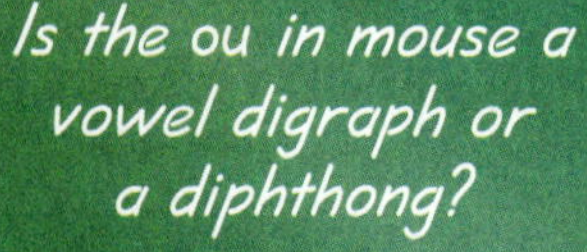

CHAPTER 3

Words, Words, Words

NOUNS

A **common noun** is the name of any person, place, or thing.

A **proper noun** names a particular person, place, or thing.

Common	Proper
girl	Melissa
park	Yellowstone National Park
day	Sunday

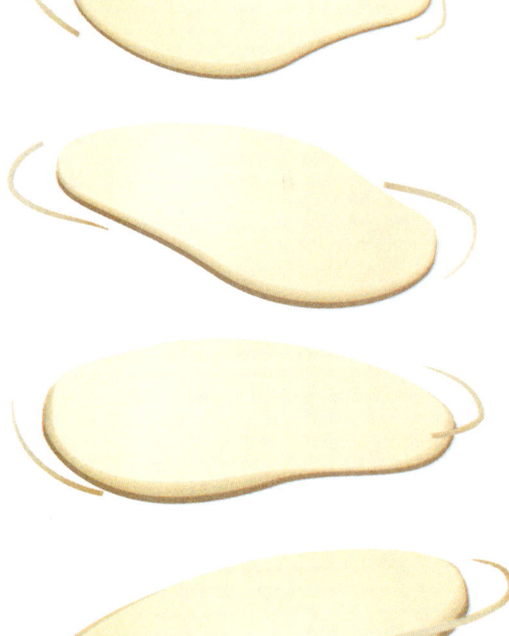

Singular nouns name one person, place, or thing.

Plural nouns name more than one person, place, or thing.

Most plural nouns end in *-s* or *-es.*

pizza**s** bush**es**

To form the plural of some nouns, special rules apply.

1. When a noun ends in *-f* or *-fe,* the *-f* is changed to *-v* and *-es* is added.

   cal**f**–cal**ves** wi**fe**–wi**ves**

   EXCEPTION: To form the plural of some nouns that end in *-f,* only an *-s* is added.

   chief–chief**s**

2. When a noun ends with a vowel plus *-o,* add *-s.*

   pat**io**–pat**ios**

3. When a noun ends with a consonant plus *-o,* add *-es.*

   pota**to**–pota**toes**

   EXCEPTION: Add an *-s* to some nouns that end with a consonant and *-o.*

   pia**no**–pia**nos**

NOUNS
PRONOUNS

4. Some plural forms are irregular.

mouse–**mice** ox–**oxen** goose–**geese**

5. Some singular and plural forms are the same.

sheep–**sheep** trout–**trout** deer–**deer**

Collective nouns name groups of people, places, things, or ideas.

team **herd** **flock**

PRONOUNS

The pronouns she and him replace the proper nouns Mary and Adam. Use pronouns to avoid repeating nouns.

A **pronoun** replaces a noun.

Mary waits for Adam. **She** wants to tell **him** something.

SINGULAR PRONOUNS	PLURAL PRONOUNS
I, me	we, us
you	you
she, he, it, her, him	they, them

A **subject pronoun** takes the place of a noun or nouns in the subject of a sentence.

Peri and **I** went to the fair. **We** ate popcorn.

An **object pronoun** follows an action verb or a word such as *at, for, to,* or *with.*

Jason threw the ball to **her.**

Samantha jumped rope with **him.**

Can you write a sentence using more than two pronouns?

SUBJECT PRONOUNS		OBJECT PRONOUNS	
Singular	**Plural**	**Singular**	**Plural**
I	we	me	us
you	you	you	you
she, he, it	they	her, him, it	them

VERBS

A **verb** is a word that expresses action or a state of being.

An **action verb** describes what the subject of a sentence has done, is doing, or will be doing. Action verbs make your writing more vivid.

She **painted** a picture. He **races** up the stairs.

The **main verb** is the most important verb in a sentence.

Jesse will be **roasting** the chicken.
main verb

A **helping verb** helps the main verb to express action.

Jesse **has** roasted the chicken.
helping verb

When the helping verb is *am, is, are, was,* or *were,* the main verb usually ends in *-ing.*

She **was walking**.

When the helping verb is *has, have,* or *had,* the main verb usually ends in *-ed.*

She **had walked**.

When the helping verb is *will,* the main verb usually does not change.

She **will walk**.

A **linking verb** connects the subject to the rest of the sentence and is usually followed by a word or words that give more information about the subject.

Melissa **is** charming. Sam **was** an officer.

The verb *is* connects the subject *Melissa* with the descriptive word *charming.* The verb *was* connects the subject *Sam* with the noun *officer.*

FORMS OF *TO BE*

Subject	Linking Verb
I	am, was
he, she, it	is, was
we, you, they	are, were

VERBS

The main verbs of a sentence can have up to three helping verbs. Write the helping verbs in the following example on paper:

He might have been promised the MVP award, but he didn't get it.

The most common of all linking verbs is a form of to be. This chart will help you figure out which form of to be you should use.

VERBS

Most **regular verbs** end in *-ed* when they are in the **past tense**.

I climb. I climb**ed**. I have climb**ed**.

Irregular verbs, such as *go*, do not end with *-ed* in the past tense.

I **go**. I **went**. I **have gone**.

SOME IRREGULAR VERBS

Present	Past	Past with Helping Verb
eat	ate	(has, have, had) eaten
give	gave	(has, have, had) given
go	went	(has, have, had) gone
say	said	(has, have, had) said
see	saw	(has, have, had) seen
sing	sang	(has, have, had) sung
take	took	(has, have, had) taken
think	thought	(has, have, had) thought

eat

ate

has eaten

Verbs have four principal parts:

1. **infinitive** to be
2. **present** I am
3. **past** I was
4. **past participle** I have been

- An **infinitive** is a regular verb preceded by the word *to*. An infinitive is often used as a noun but can be used as a verb, adjective, or adverb in a sentence.

  To wait for Jamie seems pointless. noun infinitive

  Mark wants **to play** baseball. verb infinitive

  His will **to achieve** is strong. adjective infinitive

  We eat **to live**. adverb infinitive

- A **participle** is a form of a verb.

  Present participles usually end in *-ing*.

  Past participles usually end in *-ed, -en, -d, -t,* or *-n*.

ADJECTIVES

A **common adjective** is a word that gives general information about a noun or a pronoun. **Adjectives** tell how many, which one, or what kind.

Sixty people were waiting in line.
Sixty tells how many.

Colorful balloons danced in the breeze.
Colorful tells what kind.

1. The red boat sailed across the calm water.
2. Three kittens lapped up warm milk from a blue bowl.

Demonstrative adjectives such as *this, that, these,* and *those* are used in front of nouns.

These cars are faster than **those** cars.

This hat is prettier than **that** hat.

Proper adjectives are formed from proper nouns and are always capitalized.

When a proper noun is changed to a proper adjective, the form of the noun also changes.

Swiss banks are found in **Switzerland**.
proper adjective — proper noun

1. This Italian ice tastes like the gelati we had in Italy.
2. We like French fries but have never been to France.

The adjectives *a, an,* and *the* are called **articles**. They can be definite *(the)* or indefinite *(a* or *an). The* refers to a specific person, place, thing, or idea. *A* and *an* refer to any person, place, thing, or idea.

Andy was riding **a** bike. He rode **the** blue one.
indefinite — definite

ADJECTIVES

What are the common adjectives in sentences 1 and 2? Write your answers on paper.

What are the proper nouns and proper adjectives in sentences 1 and 2? Write your answers on paper.

ADVERBS CONJUNCTIONS

ADVERBS

An **adverb** is a word that describes a verb, an adjective, or another adverb. It tells how, when, where, or how much.

The door opened **slowly**.
Slowly **tells how the door opened.**

It's **very** easy to get lost without a map.
Very **tells how much it is easy.**

Comparative adverbs are used to compare two or more actions.

The dog ran **fast**. **(describes one thing)**

The horse ran **faster**. **(compares two things)**

The gazelle ran **fastest**. **(compares three or more things)**

Adverbs make a sentence more interesting.

The turtle crawled toward the finish line.

The turtle crawled **slowly** and **surely** toward the finish line.

What adverbs would you use to make this sentence more descriptive? Write your answers on paper.

The musician _______ and ______ strummed his guitar.

CONJUNCTIONS

A **conjunction** is a word that connects a word or group of words in a sentence.

Use **and** to join words.

Ice skating **and** swimming are my favorite sports.

Use **but** to contrast two things or ideas.

I like baseball, **but** Toby likes football.

Use **or** to indicate a choice.

Would you rather go swimming **or** shopping?

PREPOSITIONS

A **preposition** is a word that connects a noun or pronoun to another word in the sentence.

Marva waited **in** the house.

She went to the store **with** me.

A preposition is followed by a noun or a pronoun that is known as the **object of the preposition**.

SOME COMMON PREPOSITIONS

about	before	except	off	to
above	behind	for	on	toward
across	beside	from	onto	under
after	between	in	out	until
along	by	inside	outside	up
around	down	into	over	upon
at	during	of	through	with

A **prepositional phrase** is made up of a preposition, the object of the preposition, and all the words in between. Prepositional phrases can be at the beginning, middle, or end of a sentence. They're easy to spot because the first word of the phrase is always a preposition.

1. **During morning assembly**, we saw a play.
2. The author **of the play** was a seventh grader.
3. It was dedicated to the writer's family.

In sentence 3, what is the prepositional phrase? What is the object of the preposition? Write your answers on paper.

INTERJECTIONS

An **interjection** is a word that shows strong feeling. It is usually followed by an exclamation point (!).

Wow! I got an A on my math test.

SOME COMMON INTERJECTIONS

Aha!	Hey!	Oh, no!	Thanks!
Great!	Hooray!	Oops!	Wow!
Help!	No way!	Ouch!	Yuck!

SENTENCES

Can you make up an example of each type of sentence? Write your sentences on paper.

SENTENCES

A **sentence** is a group of words that expresses a whole thought. It names someone or something and tells what the person or thing did.

Patsy ran for six miles.

FOUR TYPES OF SENTENCES

1. A **declarative sentence** makes a statement and ends with a period.

   Washington, D.C., is the capital of the United States.

2. An **interrogative sentence** asks a question and ends with a question mark.

   Who is your favorite music group?

3. An **imperative sentence** gives a command and ends with a period.

   Stop talking and do your homework.

4. An **exclamatory sentence** shows surprise or strong feeling and ends with an exclamation point.

   That is really cool!

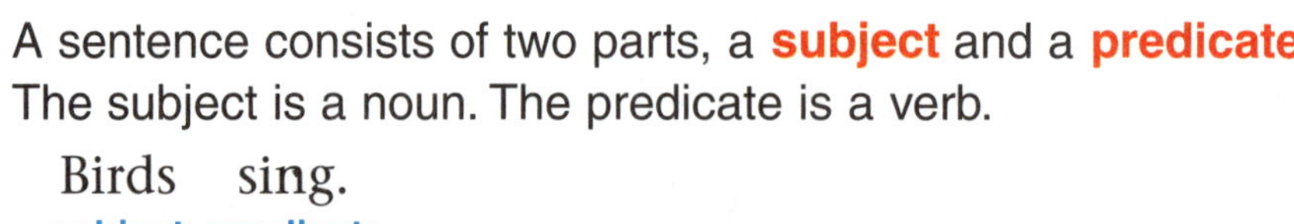

A sentence consists of two parts, a **subject** and a **predicate**. The subject is a noun. The predicate is a verb.

Birds	sing.
subject	predicate
noun	verb

The **subject** tells whom or what the sentence is about.

The **predicate** tells what the subject is or does.

The **complete subject** is all the words that make up the subject of a sentence.

The leaves on the tree fluttered in the breeze.

A **simple subject** is the main word in the complete subject.

The **leaves** on the tree fluttered in the breeze.

The **complete predicate** is all the words that make up the predicate of a sentence.

Bob **skated quickly to score a goal.**

A **simple predicate** is the main word or words in the complete predicate.

Bob **skated** quickly to score a goal.

A **compound subject** is two or more subjects that have the same predicate.

1. **Pizza** or **chicken** is the lunch choice today.
2. **Papers**, **books**, and **pencils** are in my backpack.

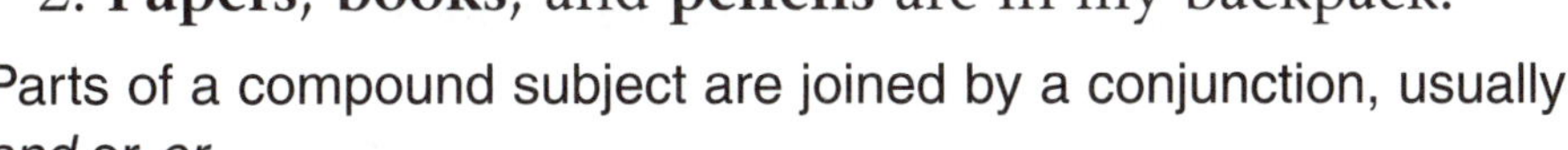

Parts of a compound subject are joined by a conjunction, usually *and* or *or*.

A **compound predicate** is two or more predicates that have the same subject.

1. He **reaches** for headphones and **puts** them on.
2. Sam wants to **play** basketball or **read** a book.

Parts of a compound predicate are joined by a conjunction.

A **compound sentence** is two or more simple sentences joined by a conjunction.

1. Gail will talk to the coach, **and** Sal will interview some players.
2. The players were nervous, **but** the coach was calm.

A **sentence fragment** is missing either a subject or a predicate and so does not express a complete thought.

1. likes apples as well as oranges
2. my brother's best friend

Make each sentence fragment into a complete thought. Write your answers on paper.

A **run-on sentence** is two or more sentences not separated by correct punctuation, capitalization, or connecting words.

1. I like to sing paint and draw Max likes to read.
2. Annemarie likes softball she plays first base.

Punctuate these run-on sentences. Write your answers on paper.

PHRASES
APPOSITIVES

PHRASES

A **phrase** is a set of two or more words that expresses a thought or idea. Phrases do not contain subjects or predicates and, therefore, are not sentences.

FOUR KIND OF PHRASES

infinitive **verb** **participial** **prepositional**

- An **infinitive phrase** contains an infinitive verb plus an adverb. Infinitive phrases begin with the word *to*.

  to drink (infinitive verb) noisily (adverb) to study (infinitive verb) hard (adverb)

- A **verb phrase** contains two or more verbs that tell about an action. It has a main verb and one or more helping verbs.

  had eaten (helping verb/main verb) should be working (helping verb/main verb)

Verb phrases containing a gerund are called **gerund phrases**. A **gerund** is a verb form that looks like a present participle (it ends in *-ing)* but acts as a noun in a sentence.

Many Western movies end with the hero **riding off into the sunset.**

- A **prepositional phrase** is a set of two or more words beginning with a preposition.

  to her **under my bed**

- A **participial phrase** is a set of two or more words that begins with a participle.

  baking cookies **jumped to conclusions**

What are the prepositional phrases in the following sentences? Write your answers on paper.

He hit the ball through the window.

She ran fast to the finish line.

APPOSITIVES

An **appositive** gives more information about a noun, pronoun, or phrase. In a sentence, an appositive comes after the noun, pronoun, or phrase it describes and is set off by commas.

My cat, **Sully**, wants to go out.

Give it to her, **the girl in yellow**, before you go.

An appositive can be left out of a sentence, and the sentence will still make sense.

CHAPTER 4

Write It, Say It, Spell It

CAPITAL LETTERS
PERIODS

CAPITAL LETTERS

Use **capital letters**:

- to begin a sentence.
  This is a cool radio station.
- for proper nouns.
  Mary Kate   Chicago   Sunday
- for proper adjectives.
  Greek   Mexican   African
- for most abbreviations.
  Jan.   Ave.   Dr.
- for words in titles, except for prepositions and articles that do not begin a title. For example: *My Side of the Mountain*.
- for the first word in the main topics and subtopics of an outline.
- in the heading, greeting, and closing of a letter.
  (see Business Letter, page 53)

PERIODS

Use a **period (.)** after:

- most initials.
  Harriet B. Stowe
- most abbreviations.
  lb. (pound)   Mon. (Monday)
- Roman numerals and uppercase letters in an outline.
  I. Australia
      A. Cities
- declarative sentences and most imperative sentences.
  We ate nachos at the movies.   Be quiet.

Greek

Mexican

African

COMMAS

COMMAS

Use a **comma (,)**:

- to separate three or more subjects in a compound subject.
  Paper, paste, glue, and buttons were used.
- to set off a quotation from the speaker. The comma is placed within the quotation marks.
  "I'm not sure," said Zack.
- after the speaker's name in a divided quotation within one sentence.
  "I'd like," shouted Marie, "a fudge sundae!"
- to separate three or more predicates in a compound predicate.
  We shouted, waved, and screamed to our friends.
- before a conjunction when it joins two simple sentences to make a compound sentence.
  We stood respectfully, and the flag was raised.
- to separate words like *yes*, *no*, and *well* from the rest of the sentence when they start a sentence.
  Yes, I am going to have lunch.
- after the name of someone who is directly addressed in a quotation.
  "Keith, are you going home?" asked Lori.
- to separate the name of the day from the date and the date from the year.
  Tuesday, March 17, 1998
- after the year when it is written with the date in the middle of a sentence.
  On Tuesday, March 17, 1998, the first meeting of the book club was held.
- to separate the names of a city and state, and after the name of a state when it's followed by other words in a sentence.
  Atlanta, Georgia
  Toni is taking a trip to Atlanta, Georgia, next month.
- after the greeting in friendly letters.
  Dear Laura,
- after the closing in both friendly and business letters.
  Very truly yours,

QUOTATION MARKS
UNDERLINES
APOSTROPHES

QUOTATION MARKS

Quotation marks (" ") are used before and after the exact words someone says. If the quotation is interrupted by other words, use quotation marks around the quoted words only.

"It's not fair!" Alex complained. "Everyone watches TV on school nights."

Quotation marks are also used around the titles of magazine articles, poems, essays, stories, and songs.

"The Worst Day of My Life" **story**

"Candle in the Wind" **song**

"The Charge of the Light Brigade" **poem**

UNDERLINES

Underline titles of books, movies, newspapers, and magazines.

<u>James and the Giant Peach</u> **book**

<u>Raiders of the Lost Ark</u> **movie**

<u>The New York Times</u> **newspaper**

<u>Newsweek</u> **magazine**

APOSTROPHES

An **apostrophe (')** takes the place of missing letters.

Use an apostrophe:

- to form contractions of pronouns and verbs.
  we're you'll I'm
- to form contractions of verbs with the word *not.*
  don't couldn't
- to form the possessive of singular and plural nouns.
  Sam's dog
  child's toy
  poems' rhymes
  photographers' awards
  children's raincoats
  sheep's wool

COLONS SEMICOLONS DASHES

COLONS

Use a **colon (:)**:

- before a list within a sentence.

  Here's what we're having: chicken, beans, rice, and pie.

- to introduce excerpts and long quotations.

  As Patrick Henry said: "I know not what course others may take, but as for me, give me liberty or give me death."

- to separate hours from minutes.

  4:00 8:15 9:45

- after the greeting of a business or formal letter.

  Dear Madam or Sir:

SEMICOLONS

A **semicolon** separates larger groupings in a sentence and indicates a longer pause than a comma.

Use a **semicolon (;)** to:

- join related independent clauses if they are not joined by a conjunction.

  The cage was empty; the bird had escaped during the night.

- to separate items in a list that are already punctuated with commas.

  This is what we need: carrots, potatoes, and lettuce; milk, juice, and soda; napkins, paper plates, and paper cups.

DASHES

A **dash** can be used:

- instead of a comma to separate interruptions in a sentence.

  My mother—as well as several other women—was selected for the committee.

- instead of a colon to separate a list from the rest of a sentence.

  Here's what to do—draft a letter, get it signed, and mail it right away.

- to indicate an interrupted statement.

  "I'm not sure that he wants one, but—"

ELLIPSES
EXCLAMATION POINTS
QUESTION MARKS

ELLIPSES

An **ellipsis (. . .)** is used:

- to replace words that have been left out in the middle of a quotation.
  "To be or not to be . . . question."
- to show that words have been omitted after the period at the end of a quotation.
  "To be or not to be, that is the question. . . ."
- to show that a list should continue in a similar pattern.
  One bug, two bugs, three bugs . . .
- to indicate an unfinished sentence or statement.
  "I was just wondering . . ."

EXCLAMATION POINTS

Use an **exclamation point (!)**:

- at the end of an exclamatory sentence.
  I won the race!
- at the end of a strong imperative sentence.
  Don't touch that!
- to separate an interjection from a sentence.
  Wow! I can't believe you ate the whole thing.

QUESTION MARKS

Use a **question mark (?)**:

- at the end of an interrogative sentence.
  Are you tired?

Punctuate these sentences. Write your answers on paper.

Hi Carrie How was your summer asked Paul

It was great replied Carrie We went swimming sailing and waterskiing What did you do this summer

I hiked to the top of Stone Mountain I also saw a lot of movies said Paul

Add the suffix -ly to these words. Write your answers on paper.

careful	*bare*
happy	*sneaky*
coy	*hearty*
sure	*gallant*

SPELLING

Here are five **basic spelling rules**. But, remember, rules usually have exceptions.

1. Ie or ei?

I before *e* **except** after *c*, or when sounding like *a* as in *neighbor* and *weigh*.

relieve

receive

EXCEPTIONS:

either

neither

height

leisure

weird

2. Final and Silent e

For words ending with a silent *-e*, drop the *-e* before adding a suffix (see page 31) that begins with a vowel.

hop**e**/hop**ing**

EXCEPTION: When the suffix begins with a consonant, do not drop the final *-e*.

hop**e**/hope**ful**

EXCEPTIONS:

acknowledg**e**/acknowledg**ment**

judg**e**/judg**ment**

3. Final y

When a word ends in a consonant and *-y*, change the *-y* to *-i* before adding a suffix.

tr**y**/tr**ied**

kindl**y**/kindl**iness**

When a word ends in a vowel and *-y*, do not change *-y* to *-i* before adding a suffix.

betra**y**/betra**yed**

emplo**y**/emplo**yment**

4. Consonant Preceded by Vowel

When a one-syllable word ends with a vowel and a single consonant, double the final consonant before adding a suffix.

ta**n**/ta**nned**

cu**t**/cu**tting**

When a word with more than one syllable ends with a vowel and a consonant, and the accent is on the last syllable, double the final consonant before adding a suffix.

patro**l**/patro**lling**

compe**l**/compe**lled**

When a word with more than one syllable ends with a vowel and a consonant, but the last syllable is **not** accented, just add a suffix to the base word.

menti**on**/menti**onable**

marv**el**/marvel**ous**

5. Double the Letter

If a prefix (see page 30) ends with the same letter with which the base word begins, include both of the repeated letters.

il + legitimate = **il**legitimate

mis + step = **miss**tep

If a suffix (see page 31) begins with the same letter with which the base word ends, include both of the repeated letters.

horizontal + ly = horizonta**lly**

thin + ness = thi**nness**

COMMONLY MISSPELLED WORDS

acceptable	counterfeit	juicy
acquaintance	disappear	license
amateur	eighth	mischief
bureau	exaggerate	nickel
calendar	flammable	parallel
cinnamon	grammar	privilege
conscience	humorous	rhythm

Correct the spellings of these words. Write your answers on paper.

accidentaly
separatly
cryed
beleive
mispelled
undoubtedlly
sprinkleing

ABBREVIATIONS
PALINDROMES

ABBREVIATIONS

An **abbreviation** is a shortened form of a word. Many abbreviations begin with a capital letter and end with a period. Others are all capital letters.

SOME ABBREVIATIONS AND WHAT THEY MEAN

C.O.D.	cash on delivery
Ave.	Avenue
Blvd.	Boulevard
mo.	month
yr.	year
lb.	pound
oz.	ounce
CD	compact disc
TV	television
VCR	video cassette recorder
ZIP	Zone Improvement Plan

PALINDROMES

A **palindrome** is a word, phrase, or sentence that is spelled the same way both forward and backward.

SOME PALINDROMES

Palindrome Words

pop nun sis noon

Palindrome Phrases

lion oil

No lemons, no melon

A Palindrome Sentence

Ma handed Edna ham.

How many other palindromes do you know? Write your answers on paper.

CHAPTER 5

Words: Where Do They Come From?

SYNONYMS
ANTONYMS

SYNONYMS

Synonyms are words whose meanings are almost the same.

stop – halt

laugh – giggle

neat – tidy

Use synonyms when writing instead of repeating the same word over again. Instead of using the word *ran* three times, here is an example using two synonyms for *ran*.

The deer **darted** into the bushes, the squirrel **scurried** up a tree, and the rabbit **ran** into its burrow.

I had an **argument** with my parents last night.

They said my room was **dirty**.

I had to stay home all **evening** and **straighten** it.

Replace the bold words in the sentences with synonyms. Write your answers on paper.

ANTONYMS

Antonyms are words whose meanings are opposite.

stop – start	multiply – divide
laugh – cry	foreign – domestic
neat – messy	boring – interesting

Using a word and its antonym in the same sentence provides contrast and makes your writing more interesting.

He cradled the **fragile** bird in his **strong** hands.

Find an antonym for each of the following words. Write your answers on paper.

huge
challenging
tired
cheerful

COMPOUND WORDS
CONTEXT CLUES

COMPOUND WORDS

A **compound word** is made up of two or more words.

THE THREE TYPES OF COMPOUND WORDS

1. **closed compound** – two words written together as one word
   examples: headache
   birthday
   everyone

2. **open compound** – two words written as separate words
   examples: dining table
   near miss
   credit card

3. **hyphenated compound** – two or more words with hyphens between them
   examples: up-to-date
   jack-in-the-box
   merry-go-round

CONTEXT CLUES

Context clues are familiar words or phrases in a sentence that help you figure out the meaning of an unfamiliar word.

He was too **miserly** to spend a single penny.

The phrase "to spend a single penny" is a context clue for *miserly*. *Miserly* means "cheap."

The **abundant** harvest meant there would be plenty of food.

The phrase "plenty of food" is a context clue for *abundant*. *Abundant* means "plentiful."

Yolanda is **elated** that she made the team, and Kerry is very happy about it, too.

What words in the sentence at the right help you figure out the meaning of elated?

HOMOPHONES

Homophones are words that sound the same but have different meanings and spellings.

Please wait **here**.
Did you **hear** the siren?

I won't **be** long.
I'm allergic to **bee** stings.

Give the key **to** me.
This drink is **too** sweet.
Josh has **two** brothers.

The tires need some **air**.
He is **heir** to the throne.

The gopher dug a **hole** in the garden.
Thomas ate a **whole** pizza.

I **need** a new coat.
You have to **knead** the bread dough.

HOMOGRAPHS

Homographs are words that are spelled the same but have different meanings. Sometimes they have different pronunciations.

Tim had to wear a **cast** on his leg.
Alexa was **cast** in the lead role.

The **train** left the station on time.
She is going to **train** for the Olympics.

I gave a **present** to my best friend.
The lawyer will **present** the case.
There is no time like the **present**.

Is that a **tear** on your cheek?
Oh! My coat has a **tear** in it.

Nora bought a **bolt** of cloth.
The lock needs a new **bolt**.
Did you see that **bolt** of lightning?
If the horse is startled, he might **bolt**.

Jeff wants to **row** across the lake.
The corn is planted in a **row**.

I need a **stamp** for the envelope.
Stamp out the fire.

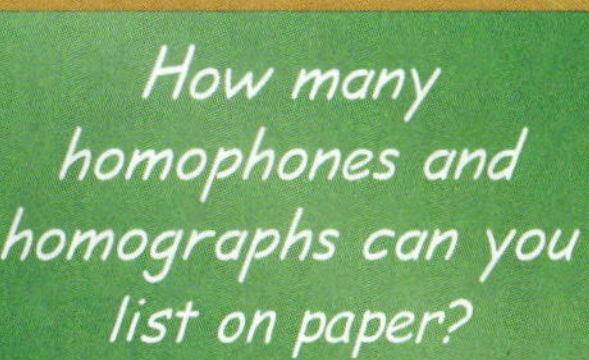

PREFIXES

PREFIXES

A **prefix** is a group of letters that is added in front of a base word to change its meaning.

A **base word** is the simplest form of a word.

Look at the box on the right. Can you find the base word in each example? Write your answers on paper.

What do the words reenact, disable, and imperfect mean? Write your answers on paper.

COMMON PREFIXES AND THEIR MEANINGS

Prefix	Meaning	Example
im-	not	impossible
ir-	not	irregular
in-	not	inactive
dis-	opposite of	disappear
mis-	incorrectly	misbehave
pre-	before	preview
re-	again; back	redo
un-	not; opposite of	unhappy
non-	not; lack of	nonsense
semi-	half; partly	semiconductor
co-	jointly	coauthor
mini-	very small	minibus
sur-	beyond	surcharge

PREFIXES THAT TELL THE NUMBER

Prefix	Meaning	Example
uni-	one	unicycle
bi-	two	bicycle
tri-	three	tricycle
deci-	ten	decimeter
centi-	hundred	centimeter
mega-	million	megabyte
giga-	billion	gigabyte

SUFFIXES

A **suffix** is a letter or group of letters added to the end of a word that changes the meaning or part of speech of the base word. Suffixes can change base words from verbs or nouns into adjectives or from verbs or adjectives into nouns.

ADJECTIVE-FORMING SUFFIXES

Suffix	Meaning	Example
-y	having; like	lucky
-ful	full of	careful
-less	without	hopeless
-able	able to be	doable
-ish	like; somewhat	impish
-ous	full	prosperous
-ways	in a certain direction	sideways
-ward	in the direction of	homeward

NOUN-FORMING SUFFIXES

Suffix	Meaning	Example
-ment	process of; state of	achievement
-ness	quality of being	wholeness
-ship	condition or state of	friendship
-er	one who	leader
-or	one who	actor
-ite	native of	suburbanite
-ism	process or act of	criticism

What does the word friendless mean?

WORD ORIGINS

WORD ORIGINS

Words become part of our language in several different ways.

1. Borrowed Words

Some English words are borrowed from other languages. For instance, the word *patio* is a Spanish word meaning "a courtyard open to the sky." *Patio* was borrowed from the Spanish to describe houses that were built with attached outdoor areas. The word now means "a recreation area that adjoins a dwelling."

SOME COMMONLY USED WORDS FROM OTHER LANGUAGES

Arabic
apricot
candy
sugar

Italian
bologna
lasagna
pasta

Spanish
avocado
burrito
chocolate

French
casserole
bouillon
omelette

Japanese
sushi
teriyaki
tofu

Yiddish
bagel
blintze
knish

2. Words from Names or Places

Many words have been adapted from proper names of people or places. For example, the word *sandwich* comes from an English earl. The 4th Earl of Sandwich (1718–1792) is believed to have come up with the idea of putting a filling between two slices of bread so he wouldn't have to stop playing cards to eat.

Braille tuxedo
leotard boycott

Where do you think these words come from? Write your answers on paper.

3. Words from Sounds

Some words have come into our language because of the sounds they describe. The word *purr* sounds very much like the sound that comes from a contented cat.

clang hiss
roar ticktock

CHAPTER 6

Tools of the Writing Trade

LITERARY DEVICES

Literary devices are techniques to help make your writing more creative, lively, and interesting. Try to use them whenever possible.

- **Alliteration**—repetition of consonant sounds, usually at the beginning of words.

  Dangerous Duo **Marvelous Monday**

- **Allusion**—references to well-known people, places, or things that are used as clues or hints to describe someone or something.

  He's a real **Einstein.** Einstein was a genius.

- **Assonance**—repetition of vowel sounds that rhyme or have the same sound.

  I saw a fl**ea** kick a tr**ee** in the middle of the s**ea**.

- **Dialogue**—words said by characters in a story. Dialogue is usually enclosed in quotation marks.

  "Little pig, little pig, let me come in," said the wolf.

- **Flashback**—description of a past event that has influenced a character's actions or feelings or brought about a present event.

- **Foreshadowing**—story elements that hint or suggest what will occur later in the story.

- **Hyperbole**—an exaggerated statement used to heighten an effect.

  I could **eat a horse.**

- **Idiomatic Expression**—an expression whose intended meaning is not the same as the literal meaning of the words.

  Watching Michael Jordan play basketball **knocks my socks off.**

LITERARY DEVICES

Allusions, similes, and metaphors are examples of imagery.

- **Imagery**—words that form a picture in a reader's mind about the way things look, sound, smell, taste, or feel.

  Her hair **shone like gold.**

- **Metaphor**—a comparison of two different things without using the words *like* or *as*.

  She has a **heart of stone.**

- **Onomatopoeia**—the use of words whose sound imitates or suggests their meaning.

  hiss **buzz** **hum** **clang** **thump**
  crash **rattle** **tinkle** **shriek** **sizzle**

- **Personification**—the giving of human characteristics to inanimate objects, animals, or ideas.

  Darkness **crept over the city.**

- **Repetition**—the intentional repeating of words, thoughts, or sounds to make writing more emphatic.

  "**I'll huff** and **I'll puff** and **I'll blow** your house down," said the wolf.

- **Simile**—a comparison of two different things using the words *like* or *as*.

  Her face was like marble.

  He was as white as a ghost.

- **Symbol**—a person, place, event, or object that suggests a meaning other than the obvious one. For example, a pig can symbolize greed.

Which literary devices are used in sentences 1-5? Write your answers on paper.

1. The baby's cheeks were **as red as apples.**
2. He **moved heaven and earth** to find her.
3. The kettle **whistled**, the pots **bubbled**, and the fire **crackled.**
4. **Betty bought buckets of butter.**
5. He never finishes, because he has his **head in the clouds.**

CHAPTER 7

Calling All Writers

THE WRITING PROCESS

Whether you're writing a song, story, poem, or report, the writing process has five steps.

THE FIVE-STEP WRITING PROCESS

1. **Prewrite** – before writing, identify your audience, think about your reason for writing and what form it will take, and make notes to organize information about your topic.
2. **Draft** – should be written from your notes. Don't worry about mistakes at this stage – the purpose is just to get all your ideas on paper.
3. **Revise and Edit** – improve, rework, and correct your first draft.
4. **Proofread** – the process of reading over your work to make sure you've made all corrections marked in the revision and editing stage.
5. **Publish** – present your work to an audience, either orally or in written form.

The first attempt to organize your ideas in writing is called a **rough draft**. When the rough draft is complete, begin to make revisions. **Revise** means to alter, amend, or correct. Even the best writers revise their work many times. Finally, you may edit your work. **Editing** is the term for polishing your final draft. After all the corrections have been made, look for places to use some of the literary devices described in Chapter 6.

While revising and editing, keep in mind the following:

REVISION CHECKLIST

1. Is your writing appropriate for your audience?
2. Does the order of sentences make sense?
3. Are there detail sentences that give more information about the topic sentence?
4. Are the sentences in logical order?
5. Have you eliminated all sentences that don't relate to the theme?
6. Have you corrected all spelling, grammar, and punctuation errors?

A **paragraph** is a group of sentences that tells about one idea. Good writing begins with effective paragraphs.

Well-written paragraphs include:

- **Topic Sentence** This introduces the theme and gives the reader an idea of what subject the paragraph discusses. The opening sentence should catch the reader's attention immediately.
- **Detail Sentences** These sentences supply more information about the theme. Use sensory details to help form a picture of what things look, sound, feel, smell, or taste like.
- **Sentence Order** Events do not have to be described in strict chronological order (the order in which something occurred), but sentences should be easy to follow.
- **Consistent Theme** Eliminate all sentences that don't relate to the theme.

Read the paragraph at the right. Write the sensory details on paper.

Thanksgiving is my favorite holiday. Outside, the air feels cool and crisp. Inside, a fire crackles, and I can smell the wonderful aroma of roasting turkey. The dining-room table is decorated with red leaves and dried ears of corn. At three o'clock, the doorbell rings. It's my grandmother with her prize-winning pumpkin pie!

Transitions are words or phrases that help connect thoughts and smoothly join sentences and paragraphs. They also help summarize or introduce conflicting ideas or events.

SOME COMMON TRANSITIONS

actually	first of all	nevertheless
again	for example	nonetheless
also	for instance	of course
but	however	otherwise
by the way	instead	secondly
finally	meanwhile	though

Tuesday is the day of the roller-blading contest. The contest begins at three o'clock and ends at four o'clock. Of course, refreshments will be served. Bring your helmet, knee pads, and wrist guards, otherwise you will not be able to participate. Make sure they are in working order. However, if you need to rent equipment, it will be available. There will be lots of spectators. By the way, the winner will appear on the six o'clock news, Tuesday night. See you then!

List the transitions. Write your answers on paper.

THE WRITING PROCESS

When revising your drafts, use these **editing symbols** – also called proofreader's marks.

PROOFREADER'S MARKS

SYMBOL	MEANING	EXAMPLE
^	add, insert	I have a ^new boombox.
℘	leave out, delete	I have a ~~new~~ boombox.
∿	transpose	She sleeps in a bed bunk.
#	insert space	She sleeps ina bunk bed.
⁀	close up space	Her name is J essica.
≡	uppercase letter	Her name is jessica.
lc	lowercase letter	Michael has a great Shot. (lc)
stet	stet, let stand	Michael has a great shot.
¶	begin new paragraph	¶ I also have a dog.
⊙	add period	His name is Moe
^,	add comma	Curly, Larry and Rosie are his friends.
‟ ”	add quotation marks	"Sit, Moe, said Curly.
:/	add colon	He can roll over, beg, and sit up.
’	add apostrophe	Moes fur is black.

Edit this paragraph using the proofreader's marks in the box.

Once upon a time, there was a a boy named Bill. He lived with his mother in a samll house.They were poor. One Day his mother said, "Jack, you must go to mar ket and sell our cow. On the way, jack met an oldman. He said hed give Jack magic beans for the cow

Graphic organizers are helpful methods for organizing information gathered during the prewriting stage. Be familiar with all of them so you can choose the one that best suits your topic.

CLUSTER DIAGRAMS

CLUSTER DIAGRAMS

A **cluster diagram** helps you remember and include details about your topic. This type of organizer is useful if you're planning to write a description of your topic.

CHARTS
VENN DIAGRAMS

CHARTS

A **chart** is useful for explaining the steps in a process. This is a good organizer for writing a how-to paragraph or article.

HOW TO MAKE A BIRD FEEDER	
Materials	plastic jug, scissors, string, birdseed
Steps	1. Clean the jug.
	2. Cut hole in side opposite handle.
	3. Tie string to handle.
	4. Fill with birdseed up to the hole.
	5. Tie jug to tree branch.
	6. Watch birds come to feast.

VENN DIAGRAMS

A **Venn diagram** is good for showing similarities and differences between two things. This is a useful organizer for comparing and contrasting.

DOGS

bark
must be walked
fetch balls

DOGS and CATS

have fur
can bite
can scratch
popular pets

CATS

meow
purr
catch mice and birds

STORY MAPS

A **story map** is helpful for planning a story or play. It's organized around a plot and reminds you to introduce the characters, setting, events, problems, climax, and resolution or conclusion.

STORY TITLE: Cinderella

CHARACTERS: Cinderella
stepmother
stepsisters
fairy godmother
prince

SETTING: fairy-tale kingdom

PROBLEM: Cinderella wants to go to the ball, but stepmother won't allow it.

EVENTS: Fairy godmother comes to Cinderella's aid.
Cinderella goes to the ball and meets the prince.
Clock strikes midnight.
Cinderella loses a glass slipper.
Prince searches kingdom to find girl whose foot fits slipper.

CLIMAX: Cinderella tries on the slipper and it fits.

CONCLUSION: Prince and Cinderella are married and live happily ever after.

CAUSE AND EFFECT DIAGRAMS OUTLINES

CAUSE AND EFFECT DIAGRAMS

A **cause and effect diagram** helps clarify relationships between two or more events.

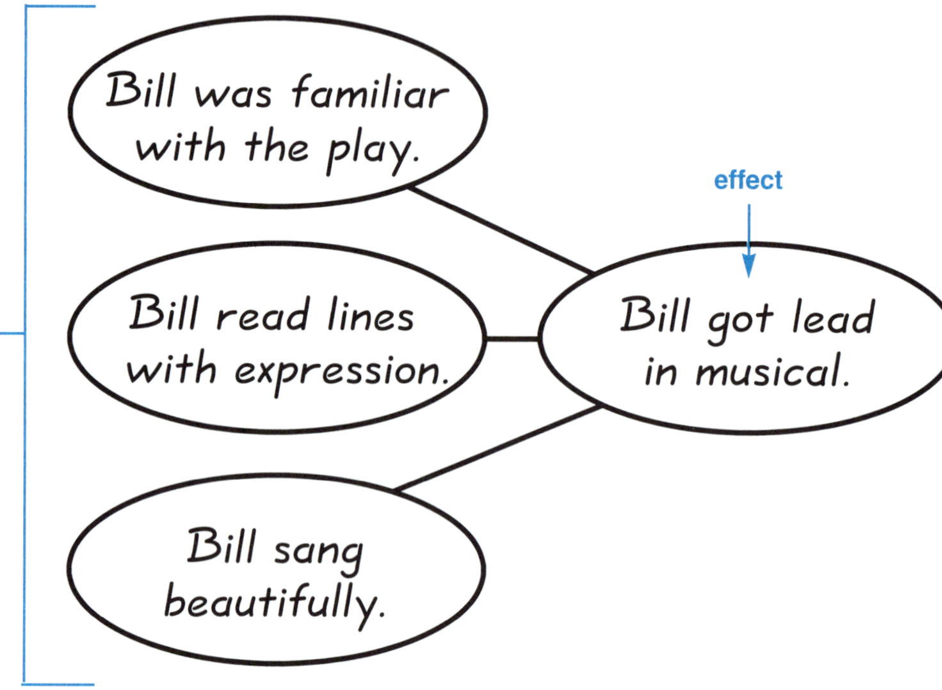

OUTLINES

An **outline** helps organize information on a broad topic with several main ideas and many details.

Outline Format:	Example:
Topic	*Basketball*
I. Main idea	*I. Origin of game*
A. Detail	*A. Idea for indoor games*
B. Detail	*B. Inventor*
C. Detail	*C. Borrowing from outdoor games*
II. Main idea	*II. Basketball today*
A. Detail	*A. Popularity in schools*
B. Detail	*B. Girls' teams*
C. Detail	*C. Basketball in the Olympics*

TIME LINES

A **time line** shows the sequence or chronological order of events.

vertical time line

INVENTIONS

3500 B.C.	Sumerians invent the wheel
300 B.C.	Euclid publishes principles of geometry
A.D. 100	Chinese invent paper
A.D. 1200	eyeglasses invented in Italy
A.D. 1400	printing press invented in Germany

horizontal time line

INVENTIONS

Sumerians invent the wheel	Euclid publishes principles of geometry	Chinese invent paper	eyeglasses invented in Italy	printing press invented in Germany
3500 B.C.	300 B.C.	A.D. 100	A.D. 1200	A.D. 1400

TIME LINES

In 2000 B.C., ice cream was invented in China. In A.D. 271, Chinese mathematicians invented the compass. Where would these events fit on the time line?

FLOW CHARTS

FLOW CHARTS

A **flow chart** also shows the steps in a process, particularly a process with a cycle. Arrows point from one event to the next until all the steps in the process are complete.

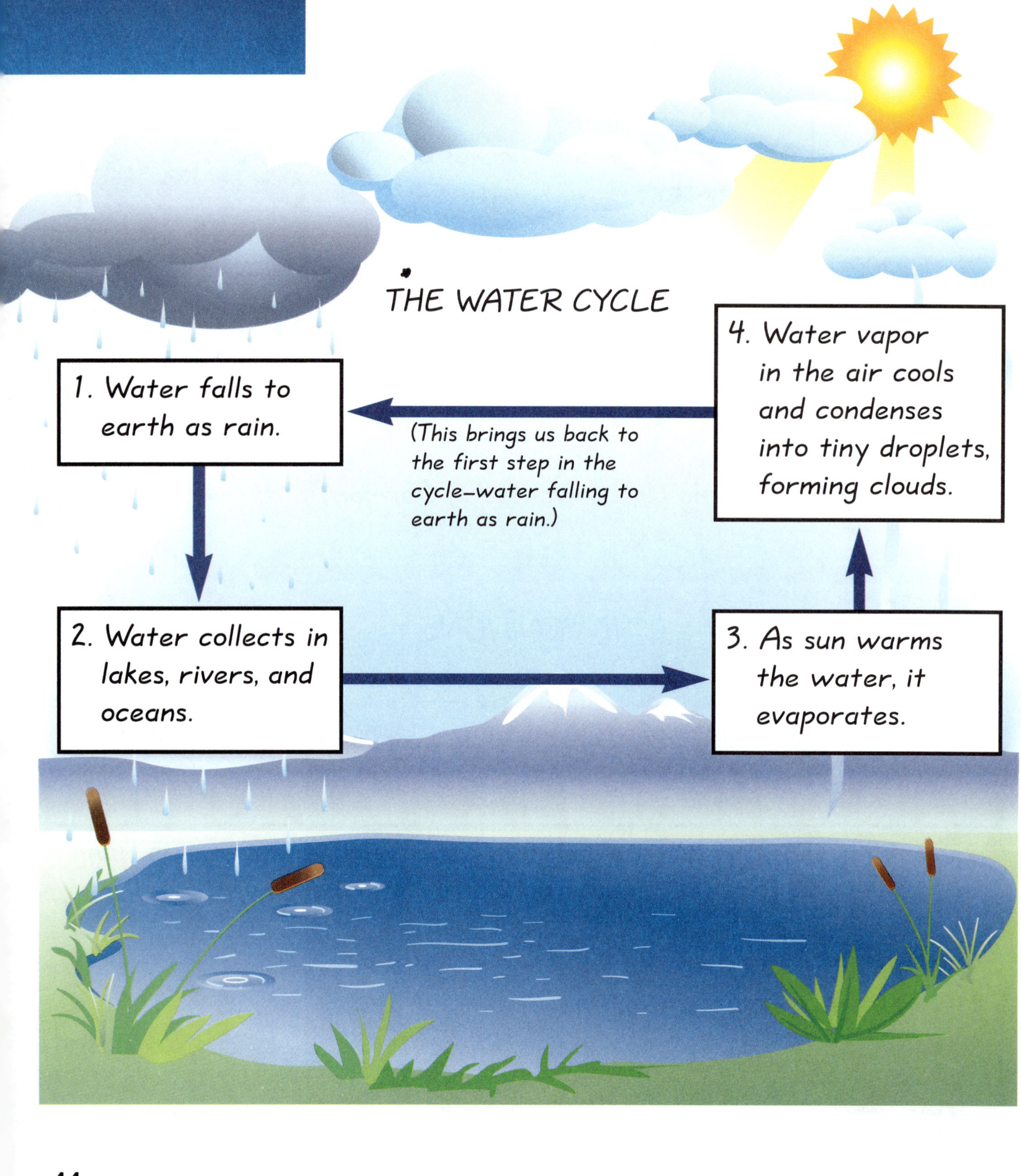

THE WATER CYCLE

1. Water falls to earth as rain.

2. Water collects in lakes, rivers, and oceans.

3. As sun warms the water, it evaporates.

4. Water vapor in the air cools and condenses into tiny droplets, forming clouds.

(This brings us back to the first step in the cycle—water falling to earth as rain.)

CHAPTER 8

All About Creative Writing

POETRY

Poems are written in lines according to different patterns (called rhyme schemes), but not all poetry is written in rhyme. Common to all forms of poetry, however, is that a feeling, idea, or story is told in rhythmic verse.

- A **ballad** is a simple and often sad story about a popular hero. Ballads usually rhyme and may be sung or spoken. (Example: "On Top of Old Smoky")
- An **epic** is a long narrative poem about the deeds of a single heroic individual or a major theme. (Example: "Casey at the Bat")
- **Haiku** is a Japanese form of poetry with a nature theme. It's usually written in the present tense and has three lines containing a total of seventeen syllables (5-7-5 rhyme scheme).

  The falling flower **5 syllables**

  I see drift back to the branch **7 syllables**

  Is a butterfly. **5 syllables**

- A **limerick** is a humorous poem of five lines with a fixed rhythm and rhyme scheme. The rhyme scheme is described as AABBA. This means the first, second, and fifth lines rhyme with one another. The third line rhymes with the fourth.

  There is a young lady whose nose **(A)**
  Continually prospers and grows; **(A)**
  When it grew out of sight, **(B)**
  She exclaimed in fright, **(B)**
  "Oh, farewell to the end of my nose." **(A)**

- A **lyric poem**, which may or may not rhyme, usually expresses a personal thought, emotion, or state of mind. Sonnets are a type of lyric poem.

POETRY
POETIC TERMS

- A **narrative poem** tells a story. The earliest narratives were creation myths, legends, or tales about historical heroes, such as Paul Bunyan.

- A **sonnet** is a lyric poem of 14 lines expressing personal thoughts or feelings of love. William Shakespeare, an English playwright and poet, wrote 154 sonnets.

Some poetry follows a strict format, such as sonnets, limericks, or haiku, while other poetry is written in a style called **free verse**. In free verse the sound of the words chosen by the poet determines when the line breaks will occur. Poems written in free verse usually don't rhyme.

Put the following types of poems in order–from shortest to longest. Write your answers on paper.

epic
haiku
limerick
sonnet

POETIC TERMS

- **Meter** is the rhythm created from emphasizing certain syllables.

  Mary had a little lamb,
  Its fleece was white as snow.

- **Rhyme** is the repetition of the same or similar sound.

  Jack and Jill went up a hill . . .
  Jack fell down and broke his crown . . .

- **Rhythm** is the arrangement of words according to their stressed and unstressed syllables.

  Little Miss Muffet sat on a tuffet . . .

- A **stanza** has two or more lines of rhymed verse that make up one section of a poem. A pattern of meter and rhyme may be repeated in each stanza. A stanza is to poetry what paragraphs are to prose.

FICTION

Fiction can be any kind of writing made up from the author's imagination. Fiction is written in **prose**, the form of everyday speech.

A **narrative** is a story. To write a narrative simply means to give an orderly account of an event.

Some of the best-known categories of fiction are:

- **Fables**—short stories that have a moral lesson. Animals or objects often speak as humans in these stories. Many fables, such as "The Fox and the Grapes," are associated with an ancient Greek slave named Aesop.
- **Fairy Tales**—stories with happy endings in which good triumphs over evil. Magical objects and transformations are common in fairy tales. "Rumpelstiltskin," by the Brothers Grimm, and "The Princess and the Pea," by Hans Christian Andersen, are well-known fairy tales.
- **Fantasy**—stories that are a combination of common events and imaginary occurrences. For example, *Charlotte's Web, Tuck Everlasting,* and *The Borrowers* are fantasy stories. Each book contains elements that could never exist in the world as we know it.
- **Folktales**—stories that have been passed down from generation to generation, in both oral and written form. Legends, tall tales, myths, fables, and fairy tales are all types of folktales.
- **Historical Fiction**—refers to stories that are based on history and that intertwine real and fictional characters. The author invents characters and settings to fit into actual historical events. *Sounder, Caddie Woodlawn,* and *Anne of Green Gables* are all historical fiction.
- **Horror**—stories that depict terrible and scary things. They usually include bloody or gory images. Monsters, ghosts, and goblins are common in horror stories.
- **Legends**—stories about real people whose characteristics have been exaggerated. The legends about King Arthur are invented stories about a king who actually lived long ago. Legends are sometimes called folklore.
- **Mysteries**—suspenseful, fast-paced stories. These books often involve someone solving a problem or a crime. *The Westing Game* is a popular mystery book.

- **Myths**—ancient stories that were devised in various cultures to explain the creation of the world and forces of nature that people did not understand. Ancient myths told of gods and goddesses who were responsible for major events in the world. *The Odyssey* is an example of a myth.
- **Realistic Fiction**—refers to stories that have been made up, but the events and characters are so believable that the reader imagines the stories could be true. *The Moffats, All-of-a-Kind Family*, and *The Summer of the Swans* are examples of realistic fiction.
- **Romances**—stories in which the main characters search for love and happiness. Sometimes, these books are set in historical times.
- **Science Fiction**—a type of fantasy story. Often set in the future, these books use scientific facts and hypotheses to create exciting action stories. Space, biotechnology, and computers often play a part in science fiction. *Long After Midnight,* by the noted writer Ray Bradbury, is an example of science fiction.
- **Tall Tales**—stories that have been greatly exaggerated or made up. Tall tales are told about imaginary characters, such as Paul Bunyan, or real heroes, such as Davy Crockett.

NONFICTION

Nonfiction is writing based on actual events—either current or historical. Nonfiction is also written in prose.

Some of the best-known categories of nonfiction are:

- **Autobiography**—a story of a person's life that has been written by that person. An example is *Anne Frank, Diary of a Young Girl.*
- **Biography**—this is also the story of a person's life, but it has been written by someone else. The writer of a biography is called a biographer. Often, biographies are about prominent individuals: for example, *Colin Powell,* by Jim Haskins.
- **Informational books**—books about a particular category or subject. If you are interested in mammals or space travel, you might choose an informational book on that subject. *How Did We Find Out About Outer Space?,* by Isaac Asimov, or *Pyramid,* by David Macaulay, are informational books.

ELEMENTS OF A STORY

- **Point of view** is the author's choice of narrator or speaker in a story. The author's choice of point of view determines how much information the reader will be given. In **first person point of view**, the main character in the story is the narrator and uses the word *I* when speaking. The reader learns the narrator's thoughts and feelings and finds out about the other characters and the events of the story through the main character's eyes. **Third person point of view** also tells the reader what the characters in the story are thinking, but it uses a voice from outside the story. This narrator describes all the characters and their actions using the pronouns *she*, *her*, *he*, *him*, *they*, or *them*.
- **Characters** are the people in a story. A character's actions, motives, and feelings help determine the action—and often the meaning—of the story. We get to know the characters by what they do, feel, and say. The **protagonist**, or main character, is usually the hero or heroine and the one whose actions are followed throughout the plot. The **antagonist** is often the villain or the protagonist's opponent.
- The **plot** is what happens in the story. Most plots involve a character's attempts to reach a goal and the result of those attempts. A **subplot** is a secondary story that is interwoven into the main plot.
- **Exposition** is introductory or background information that the reader needs to know in order to understand what is happening.
- The **climax** of a story is its high point, where the reader is most emotionally involved in the character's attempts to reach a goal and where the complexities of a story are resolved.
- The **theme** of a story is the main idea or point the author is trying to make.
- The **setting** is exactly when and where the story occurs. This means establishing not only the time in history the event takes place, but also the time of day, month, or year. Information about the actual geographic location of the story is also included.

- **Mood** is the atmosphere or feeling of a story, which may change as the story progresses. The mood may be thoughtful, happy, dreamlike, sad, and so forth. There are moods for every human emotion.

  "The woods are lovely, dark, and deep . . . "

- Authors use **tone** to create the mood of a story. Tone is the feeling or mood established by the choice of words. A tone can be gentle, cheerful, sad, rousing, gloomy, harsh, and so forth.

  "And the rockets red glare,
  The bombs bursting in air . . ."

STORY STRUCTURE

The following questions and answers about *Charlie and the Chocolate Factory* by Roald Dahl use the story elements introduced above to help analyze the story structure:

1. Who is the main character, or **protagonist**?

   Charlie Bucket

2. Who are the **antagonists**?

   Augustus Gloop, Veruca Salt, Violet Beauregarde, Mike Teavee, and at the beginning Willy Wonka

3. What is the **plot**?

   Charlie wins a chance to enter a special chocolate factory.

4. What is the **setting**?

   the chocolate factory

5. What is the **climax**?

   Charlie is the only child left in the chocolate factory. He becomes the owner of the factory.

6. What is the **theme**?

   Goodness triumphs over evil.

PLAYS

A **play** is a story written to be performed on a stage in front of an audience. The author of a play is called a **playwright**. Plays have the same basic elements as other stories—characters, setting, plot, and theme. **Stage directions**, also written by the playwright, give information about the setting and instructions to the actors about what to do onstage as they say their lines.

Plays are divided into **acts** (usually a play has one, two, or three acts). Within each act there are **scenes**, even smaller units of time and setting, used to develop the action and the characters of that act.

A **narrator** sometimes introduces a play and explains what is happening at certain points.

Some of the best-known types of plays are:

- **Tragedy**—a serious play, often with an unhappy ending. In classical theater, tragedies often describe the death or downfall of noble persons. A famous Greek tragedy is *Oedipus Rex,* by Sophocles. Shakespearean tragedies include *Hamlet, Macbeth,* and *Othello. The Death of a Salesman* is a modern tragedy written by the American playwright Arthur Miller.
- **Comedy**—a humorous play with a happy ending. Comedies sometimes include slapstick, farce, and satire. *Frogs,* by Aristophanes, a Greek playwright, is a classical comedy. William Shakespeare wrote many comedies, including *A Midsummer Night's Dream* and *Twelfth Night. The Odd Couple* and *Barefoot in the Park* are modern American comedies written by Neil Simon.
- **Musical**—a play that includes songs, dialogue, and sometimes dancing. Although most modern musicals are comedies, sometimes musicals have serious endings. In a musical, the playwright writes the text, the composer writes the music, and the lyricist writes the words to the songs—sometimes a single person does more than one of these jobs. The composer Richard Rodgers worked with the lyricist Oscar Hammerstein II to create many famous musicals, such as *Oklahoma, The King and I,* and *The Sound of Music.*

LETTERS

LETTERS

There are two main types of letters: In a **friendly letter**, the writer is sending greetings or news to someone she or he knows—usually a friend or relative. There are five parts to a friendly letter.

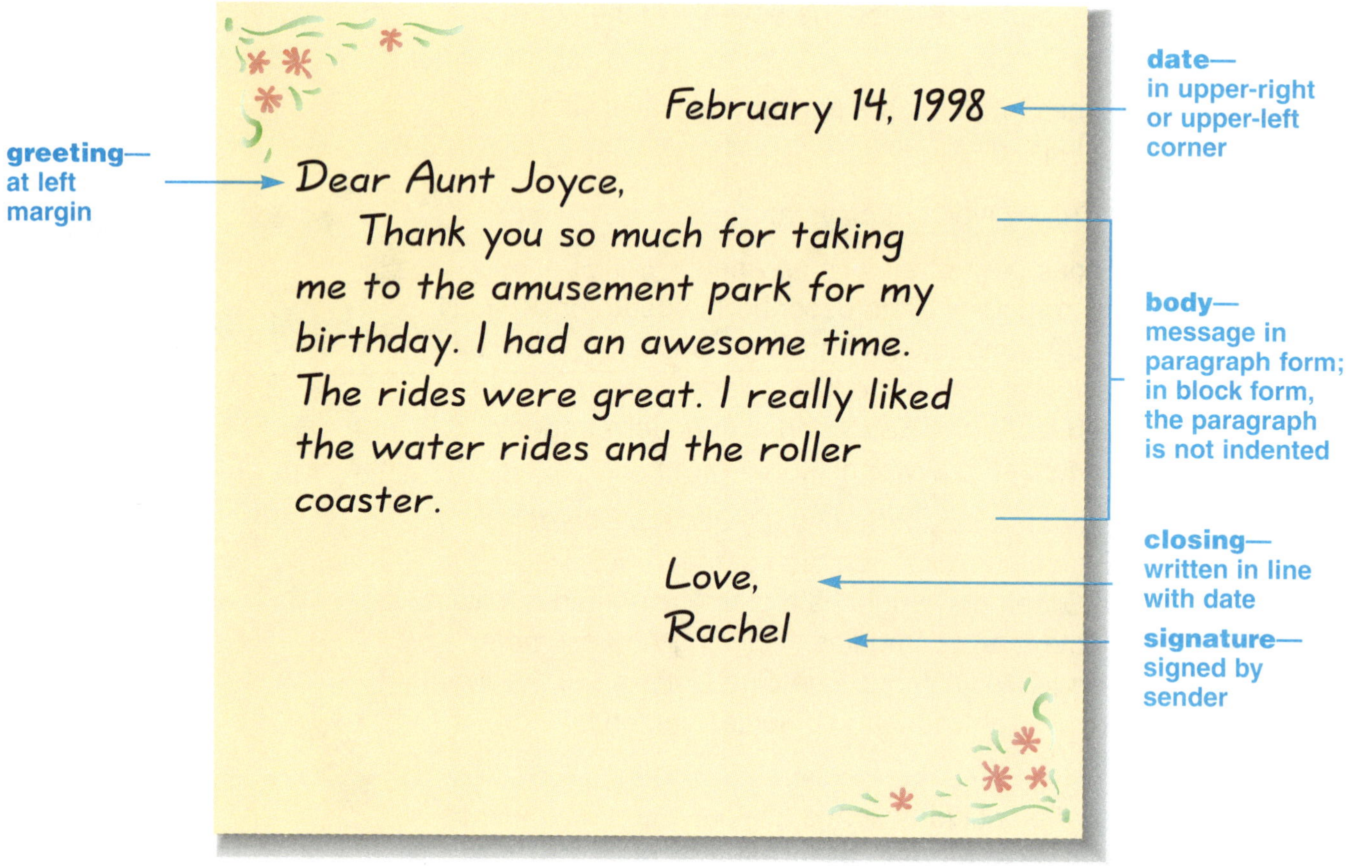

February 14, 1998

Dear Aunt Joyce,

Thank you so much for taking me to the amusement park for my birthday. I had an awesome time. The rides were great. I really liked the water rides and the roller coaster.

Love,

Rachel

greeting—at left margin

date—in upper-right or upper-left corner

body—message in paragraph form; in block form, the paragraph is not indented

closing—written in line with date

signature—signed by sender

In a **business letter**, the writer is often writing to someone she or he doesn't know. Usually the business letter asks for or provides information. A business letter has six parts.

The heading of a business letter includes your own (the sender's) address as well as the recipient's name and address.

Use a colon after the greeting in a business letter instead of a comma.

Appropriate closings are:

Yours truly, Very truly yours, Sincerely, *or* Sincerely yours.

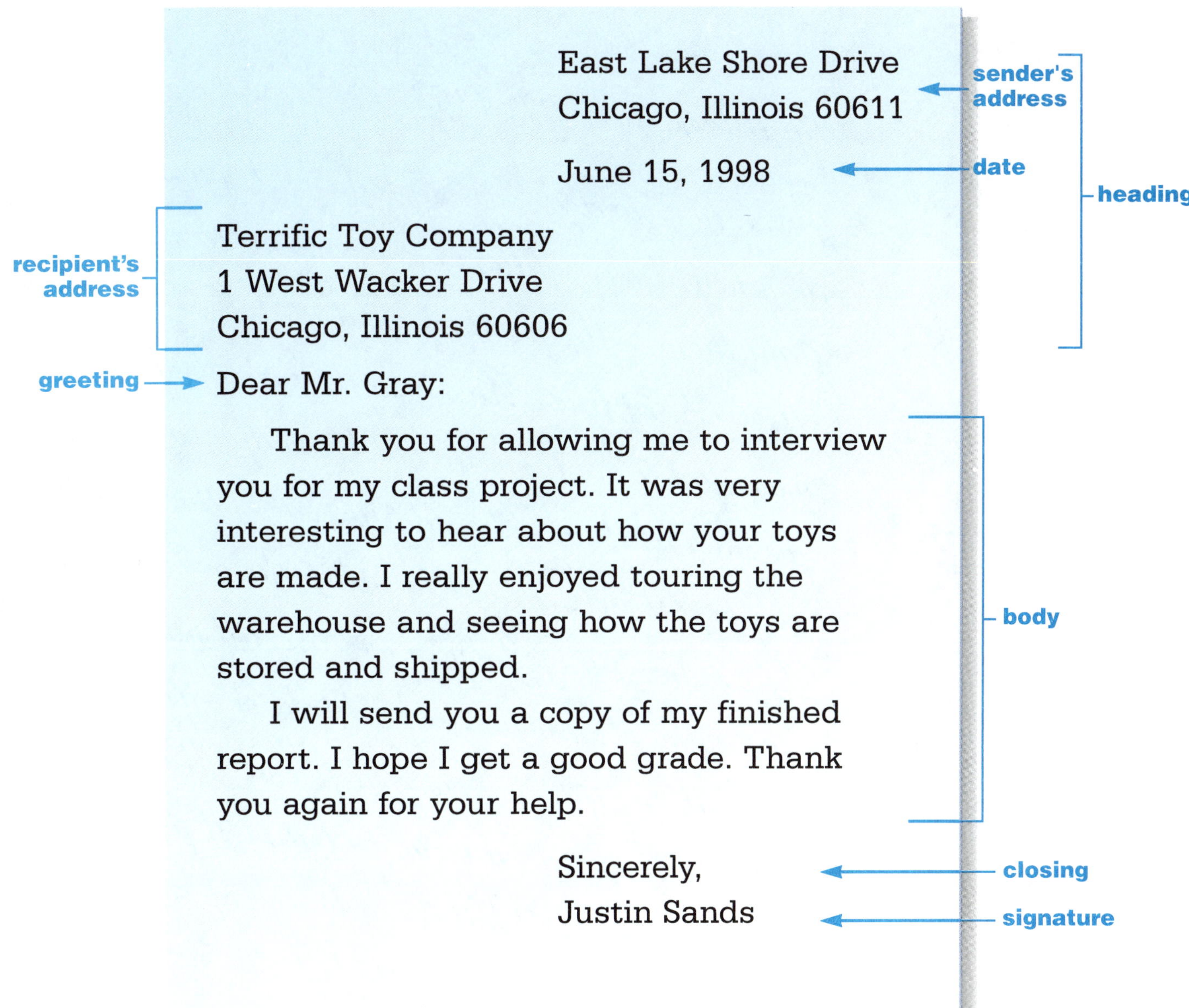
East Lake Shore Drive
Chicago, Illinois 60611

June 15, 1998

Terrific Toy Company
1 West Wacker Drive
Chicago, Illinois 60606

Dear Mr. Gray:

Thank you for allowing me to interview you for my class project. It was very interesting to hear about how your toys are made. I really enjoyed touring the warehouse and seeing how the toys are stored and shipped.

I will send you a copy of my finished report. I hope I get a good grade. Thank you again for your help.

Sincerely,
Justin Sands

JOURNALS

JOURNALS

A **journal** or diary is a daily record of events, thoughts, and feelings written by a person for his or her own use. *Amelia's Journal,* by Marissa Moss, and *Anne Frank: The Diary of a Young Girl* are examples.

We can learn much about what happened in the past from reading journals—even those kept by young people. The following is an entry made by a girl named Rebecca who lived in the small town of Gettysburg, Pennsylvania, during the Civil War.

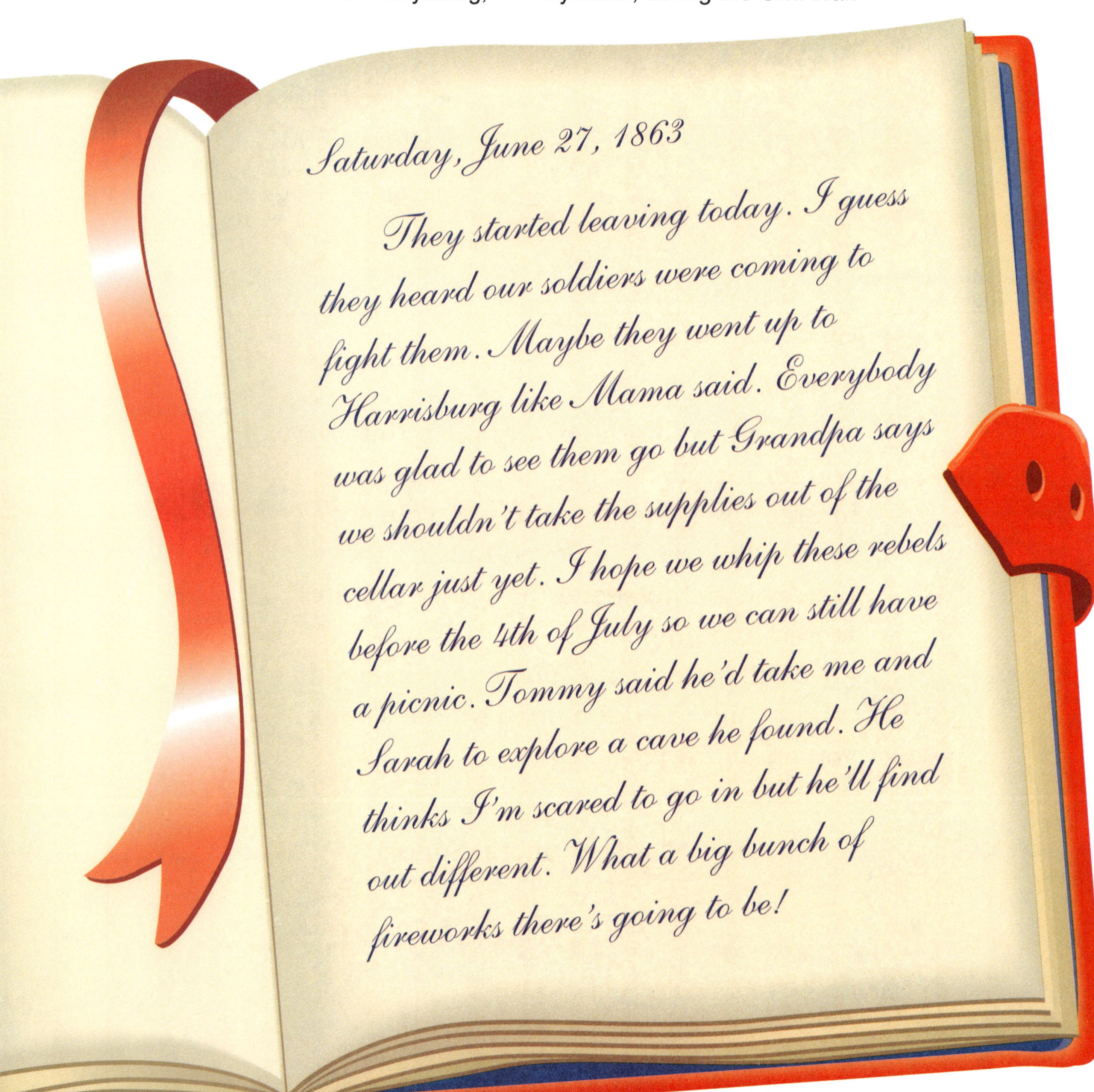

The Right Source

Knowing what reference material to use when doing research not only will save you time, but also will provide you with the most complete and current information for your project.

USING THE LIBRARY

Library material from the Reference section cannot be checked out; it must be used in the library. This includes encyclopedias, atlases, indexes, dictionaries, thesauruses, directories, and current newspapers and magazines. Older magazine or newspaper articles, usually on microfilm or microfiche (a photographic record), are read through a viewer. One of the best resources in the library is the **librarian**. Don't hesitate to ask your librarian for suggestions when conducting your research.

REFERENCE SOURCES

- An **almanac**, published yearly, contains calendars, information about weather, holidays, hours of sunrise and sunset, news events from the previous year, populations of cities, charts and tables, and lists on a variety of subjects.
- An **atlas** is a book of maps. Some research topics (such as agriculture, politics, or exploration) are affected by geography. For these projects an atlas is very useful. There are special atlases that show maps of the world as it was in historical times.

REFERENCE SOURCES

Write a bibliography entry for the following information:

Dear Mr. Henshaw is a book written by Beverly Cleary and published in Boston by Houghton Mifflin in 1995.

- A **bibliography** is a list of books or articles used as sources for researching a topic. Bibliographies usually are organized alphabetically by the authors' last names or by the titles of the sources.

  Lawson, Robert. *Ben and Me*. New York: Little Brown, 1988.
  author, last name first | title of book | city | publisher | publication year

  Buy Me That. Consumer's Union Films, Inc. (VHS video, 1989).
  videotape title | name of publisher | type of video | publication year

  Silver, Michael. "Rush to the Super Bowl." *Sports Illustrated*. Dec. 29, 1997, page 32.
  author, last name first | title of article | magazine | issue date | page

- An **encyclopedia** can be one book on a single subject (such as music or art) or part of a complete set. Each book in a set is called a volume. General encyclopedias contain information on many subjects, all arranged alphabetically.

- A **newspaper** contains local, national, and/or international news. It can be published daily, weekly, or semimonthly.

- A **periodical** is a magazine or other regularly issued publication. *The Readers' Guide to Periodical Literature* lists articles published in periodicals. The listings are arranged alphabetically, either by author, by subject, or by title. The magazine name, issue, and pages on which the article appeared are given. This is an excellent reference tool for researching a current subject.

- A **thesaurus** is a special dictionary in which synonyms, antonyms, and other related words are classified. A thesaurus helps writers avoid using the same words over again.

- A **vertical file** in the library contains non-book items, such as brochures and pamphlets.

- The **card catalog** is an alphabetical listing of all books in the library—either by subject, by author, or by title. (In most libraries, the card catalog is now on computer.)

- A **dictionary** is a book that lists words, also called **entries**, in alphabetical order along with their definitions and pronunciations. A dictionary also tells what part of speech a word is and how to form the plural.

To look up a dictionary entry, note the two **guide words** at the top of each page. Only words that fall alphabetically between the guide words will be on the page.

If there is more than one definition or meaning for a word, read them all until you find the one you need.

A variation in spelling follows the preferred spelling.

Word divisions show how the entry word is divided into two or more **syllables**, a word part that contains only one vowel sound.

The **phonetic respelling** indicates how an entry word is pronounced. Phonetic respellings are also divided into syllables.

An **accent mark** indicates how much emphasis to place on each syllable. If a word has two accents, the stressed syllable has the bolder mark or **primary accent**. The other accent mark is the **secondary accent**.

A **pronunciation key**, usually found at the beginning of the dictionary, explains the symbols used in phonetic respellings.

Homographs, words that are spelled the same but have different meanings, have separate entries.

If the guide words on a dictionary page are green and grief, which of the following words would be on that page? Write your answers on paper.

greet
grim
grew
great
griddle
grit
greenhouse
grill

REFERENCE SOURCES
THE COMPUTER AS A REFERENCE TOOL

HELPFUL HINTS FOR WRITING A RESEARCH PAPER

- At your local or school library, look up the general topic you are researching. Check the card catalog for specific books or authors.
- Remember that magazine and newspaper articles can be helpful.
- Use the encyclopedia to get general information. Look at a computer encyclopedia or search the Internet.
- Take careful notes. Write down the name and page numbers of the books you use. Attribute direct quotes. Remember to use quotation marks.
- Take notes on 5x7 index cards so that it is easier to order the information for your report.
- Keep a list of the sources you use so that you can write a bibliography.
- Don't be shy—ask a librarian, teacher, parent, or friend for help.

THE COMPUTER AS A REFERENCE TOOL

Many public and school libraries now use **computers** for their card catalog files and research materials.

Encyclopedias, thesauruses, dictionaries, and atlases are now all stored on **CD-ROMS**. Using a CD-ROM allows encyclopedias and other reference works to fit on a single disc. To use this kind of reference guide, a computer equipped with a CD-ROM drive is needed. The user then just scrolls through the "find" or "search" screen alphabetically until the desired information is found.

Many schools, homes, and libraries are now connected to the World Wide Web via an Internet provider. Using a web browser, you surf the net to find topics of interest. An E-mail address allows one to communicate all over the world via the Internet at a fraction of the cost of a phone call.

REALISTIC FICTION

Cormier, Robert. *The Chocolate War.* New York: Bantam Doubleday Dell, 1986.
Creech, Sharon. *Walk Two Moons.* New York: HarperCollins, 1994.
Danziger, Paula. *The Cat Ate My Gymsuit.* New York: Bantam Doubleday Dell, 1980.
Holub, Josef. *The Robber and Me.* New York: Henry Holt & Company, Inc., 1997.
Konigsburg, E. L. *The View from Saturday.* New York: Simon & Schuster, 1996.
L'Engle, Madeleine. *A Ring of Endless Light.* New York: Bantam Doubleday Dell, 1981.
Lowry, Lois. *Anastasia Krupnick.* Boston: Houghton Mifflin, 1979.
Paterson, Katherine. *Jacob Have I Loved.* New York: Avon Books, 1981.
Snyder, Zilpha K. *The Gypsy Game.* New York: Bantam Doubleday Dell, 1997.
Spinelli, Jerry. *Crash.* New York: Alfred A. Knopf, 1997.

HISTORICAL FICTION

Brink, Carol R. *Caddie Woodlawn.* New York: Simon & Schuster, 1990.
Collier, James L. *The Clock.* New York: Bantam Doubleday Dell, 1995.
Collier, James L., and Christopher Collier. *My Brother Sam Is Dead.* New York: Simon & Schuster, 1984.
Hautzig, Esther. *The Endless Steppe.* New York: HarperCollins, 1987.
Magorian, Michelle. *Good Night, Mr. Tom.* New York: HarperCollins, 1986.
O'Dell, Scott. *Streams to the River, River to the Sea: A Novel of Sacagawea.* Boston: Houghton Mifflin, 1986.
Van Leeuwen, Jean. *Bound for Oregon.* New York: Dial Books for Young Readers, 1994.

FANTASY

Babbitt, Natalie. *Tuck Everlasting.* New York: Farrar, Straus and Giroux, 1985.
Banks, Lynne Reid. *The Indian in the Cupboard.* New York: Avon Books, 1982.
Carroll, Lewis. *Alice's Adventures in Wonderland.* New Jersey: Troll Communications, 1993.
Juster, Norton. *The Phantom Tollbooth.* New York: Random House, 1988.
Lewis, C. S. *The Lion, the Witch, and the Wardrobe.* New York: HarperCollins, 1994.
O'Brien, Robert C. *Mrs. Frisby and the Rats of NIMH.* New York: Simon & Schuster, 1986.
Rodgers, Mary. *Freaky Friday.* New York: HarperCollins, 1973.

ADVENTURE

Avi. *The True Confessions of Charlotte Doyle.* New York: Avon Books, 1992.
Fleischman, Sid. *The Whipping Boy.* New Jersey: Troll Communications, 1996.
Hinton, S. E. *The Outsiders.* New York: Viking Penguin, 1997.
Konigsburg, E. L. *Up from Jericho Tel.* New York: Simon & Schuster, 1986.
Norton, Mary. *The Borrowers.* New York: Harcourt Brace & Company, 1993.
O'Dell, Scott. *Island of the Blue Dolphins.* New York: Bantam Doubleday Dell, 1996.
Paulsen, Gary. *The Haymeadow.* New York: Bantam Doubleday Dell, 1994.
Stevenson, Robert Louis. *Treasure Island.* New Jersey: Troll Communications, 1980.

SCIENCE FICTION AND THE SUPERNATURAL

Bradbury, Ray. *Long After Midnight.* New York: Alfred A. Knopf, 1976.

Du Bois, William P. *The Twenty-One Balloons.* New York: Puffin Books, 1986.

Grahame, Kenneth. *The Wind in the Willows.* New Jersey: Troll Communications, 1992.

L'Engle, Madeleine. *A Wrinkle in Time.* New York: Bantam Doubleday Dell, 1996.

Lowry, Lois. *The Giver.* New York: Bantam Doubleday Dell, 1994.

Nixon, Jean L. *A Deadly Game of Magic.* New York: Bantam Doubleday Dell, 1985.

Raskin, Ellen. *The Westing Game.* New York: Puffin Books, 1992.

POETRY

Silverstein, Shel. *A Light in the Attic.* New York: HarperCollins, 1981.

Viorst, Judith. *If I Were in Charge of the World and Other Worries: Poems for Children and Their Parents.* New York: Simon & Schuster, 1984.

Volavkova, Hana (ed.). *I Never Saw Another Butterfly: Children's Drawings and Poems from Terezin Concentration Camp 1942–1944.* New York: Pantheon Books, 1993.

INFORMATIONAL

Barkin, Carol, and Elizabeth James. *Jobs for Kids.* New York: Lothrop, Lee & Shepard, 1990.

———*The New Complete Babysitter's Handbook.* Boston: Houghton Mifflin, 1995.

Fritz, Jean. *Shh! We're Writing the Constitution.* New York: Putnam, 1987.

James, Elizabeth, and Carol Barkin. *Sincerely Yours: How to Write Great Letters.* Boston: Houghton Mifflin, 1993.

Lester, Julius. *To Be a Slave.* New York: Dial Books for Young Readers, 1968.

Macaulay, David. *The Way Things Work.* Boston: Houghton Mifflin, 1988.

Maestro, Betsy C. *The Voice of the People: American Democracy in Action.* New York: Lothrop, Lee & Shepard, 1996.

BIOGRAPHY AND AUTOBIOGRAPHY

Cleary, Beverly. *A Girl from Yamhill: A Memoir.* New York: Avon Books, 1996.

Dahl, Roald. *Boy: Tales of Childhood.* New York: Puffin Books, 1986.

Fritz, Jean. *And Then What Happened, Paul Revere?* New York: Putnam, 1996.

Krull, Kathleen. *Lives of the Writers: Comedies, Tragedies (and What the Neighbors Thought).* New York: Harcourt Brace & Company, 1994.

Stanley, Diane. *Leonardo da Vinci.* William Morrow & Company, 1996.

PAGE 7

Answers will vary. Possible answers include:
Initial: brown, plane
Medial: celebrate, control
Final: lamp, left

PAGE 8

diphthong

PAGE 10

Answers will vary. Possible answers include:
She ran to give him his ball.

PAGE 11

might have been

PAGE 13

common adjectives:
1. red, calm
2. three, warm, blue

proper nouns: Italy, France

proper adjectives: Italian, French

PAGE 14

Answers will vary. Possible answers include:
gently, softly

PAGE 15

prepositional phrase: to the writer's family

object of the preposition: family

PAGE 16

Answers will vary. Possible answers include:
Declarative: Ice cream is my favorite food.
Interrogative: Did you do your homework?
Imperative: Shut the door.
Exclamatory: This was a fabulous concert!

PAGE 17

Answers will vary. Possible answers include:

sentence fragment:
1. Denise likes apples as well as oranges.
2. Max is my brother's best friend.

run-on sentences punctuated:
1. I like to sing, paint, and draw. Max likes to read.
2. Annemarie likes softball. She plays first base.

PAGE 18

prepositional phrases:
through the window
to the finish line

PAGE 23

"Hi, Carrie. How was your summer?" asked Paul.
"It was great," replied Carrie. "We went swimming, sailing, and waterskiing. What did you do this summer?"
"I hiked to the top of Stone Mountain. I also saw a lot of movies," said Paul.

PAGE 24

carefully, happily, coyly, surely, barely, sneakily, heartily, gallantly

PAGE 25

accidentally, separately, cried, believe, misspelled, undoubtedly, sprinkling

PAGE 26

Answers will vary. Possible answers include:
pip, pup, Madam I'm Adam,
Too hot to hoot.

PAGE 27

Answers will vary. Possible answers include:
synonyms: fight, grimy, night, tidy
antonyms: tiny, easy, energetic, sad

PAGE 28

very happy

PAGE 29

Answers will vary. Possible answers include:
some homophones:

awl–all	flour–flower
bell–belle	floe–flow
boll–bowl	gamble–gambol
carol–carrel	hair–hare
crummy–crumby	jam–jamb
faint–feint	knot–not
flew–flue	led–lead
flea–flee	made–maid

mane–main
mite–might
pale–pail
red–read
see–sea
sic–sick
site–sight
so–sew
tee–tea
tic–tick
toe–tow
wail–whale
ware–wear
whoa–woe

some homographs:

ring
pitch
right
left
scale
watch
check
plain
company
coach
charge
catch
bowl
lie

PAGE 30

Box 1. possible, regular, active, appear, behave, view, do, happy, sense, conductor, author, bus, charge

Box 2. reenact–act again
disable–not able
imperfect–not perfect

PAGE 31

without friends

PAGE 32

Braille—Louis Braille was a French teacher of the blind.

leotard—the *leotard* was named after the French gymnast, J. Leotard.

tuxedo—the *tuxedo* was named after a suit of clothes that was worn at a country club at Tuxedo Park, New York.

boycott—Captain C. C. Boycott was a British land agent.

PAGE 34

1. simile and imagery
2. hyperbole
3. onomatopoeia
4. alliteration
5. idiomatic expression

PAGE 36

cool; crisp; crackles; aroma; roasting; red; dried; rings; pumpkin

PAGE 37

Of course; otherwise; However; By the way

PAGE 38

Once upon a time, there was a a boy named Bill. He lived with his mother in a samll house. They were poor. One Day his mother said, "Jack you must go to market to sell our cow. On the way, jack met an oldman. He said hed give Jack magic beans for the cow

Jack the

PAGE 39

Answers will vary.

PAGE 43

2000 B.C., ice cream invented in China, positions between 3500 B.C. and 300 B.C.

A.D. 271, Chinese mathematicians invent compass, positions between A.D. 100 and A.D. 1200.

PAGE 46

haiku (3 lines), limerick (5 lines), sonnet (14 lines), epic (more than 14 lines)

PAGE 56

Cleary, Beverly. *Dear Mr. Henshaw.* Boston: Houghton Mifflin, 1995.

PAGE 57

greet, grew, griddle, greenhouse